Skating

by Martha Wood
illustrated by Diane Paterson

Core Decodable 78

McGraw Hill Education

Bothell, WA • Chicago, IL • Columbus, OH • New York, NY

MHEonline.com

Send all inquiries to:
McGraw-Hill Education
8787 Orion Place
Columbus, OH 43240

ISBN: 978-0-02-132186-5
MHID: 0-02-132186-8

Printed in China

6 7 8 9 10 DSS 27 26 25 24 23

Some kids skate on ice.

Some kids skate on pavement.

Kay takes lessons at City Center.
She always skates in fancy circles.

Aiden also ice skates.

His aim is to be fast, not fancy.

Since Ray was three, he has skated.

He sails down the pavement on skates.

At some places, Gail races on ice.
At some places, Gail races on pavement.
Stay out of her way!

These kids skate all day.
Have you had a chance to skate?